Test # 198791

Level 3.1

Points 0.5

3-D PRINTERS

by Debbie Vilardi

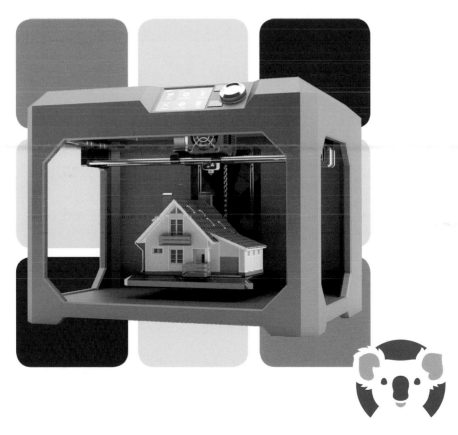

Cody Koala

An Imprint of Pop!
popbooksonline.com

abdopublishing.com

Published by Pop!, a division of ABDO, PO Box 398166, Minneapolis, Minnesota 55439. Copyright © 2019 by POP, LLC. International copyrights reserved in all countries. No part of this book may be reproduced in any form without written permission from the publisher. Pop!™ is a trademark and logo of POP, LLC.

Printed in the United States of America, North Mankato, Minnesota

042018
092018

THIS BOOK CONTAINS
RECYCLED MATERIALS

Distributed in paperback by North Star Editions, Inc.

Cover Photo: iStockphoto
Interior Photos: iStockphoto, 1, 6, 10 (top), 10 (bottom), 14, 17, 21; Shutterstock Images, 5 (top), 5 (bottom left), 5 (bottom right), 9 (top), 9 (bottom left), 9 (bottom right), 10 (middle), 13; Chelsea Purgahn/Tyler Morning Telegraph/AP Images, 18

Editor: Charly Haley
Series Designer: Laura Mitchell

Library of Congress Control Number: 2017963435

Publisher's Cataloging-in-Publication Data

Names: Vilardi, Debbie, author.
Title: 3-d printers / by Debbie Vilardi.
Description: Minneapolis, Minnesota : Pop!, 2019. | Series: 21st century inventions |Includes online resources and index.
Identifiers: ISBN 9781532160387 (lib.bdg.) | ISBN 9781635177893 (pbk) | ISBN 9781532161506 (ebook) |
Subjects: LCSH: Three-dimensional printing--Juvenile literature. | Technological innovations--Juvenile literature. | Inventions--History--Juvenile literature. | Technology--History--Juvenile literature.
Classification: DDC 609--dc23

Hello! My name is
Cody Koala

Pop open this book and you'll find QR codes like this one, loaded with information, so you can learn even more!

Scan this code* and others like it while you read, or visit the website below to make this book pop.

popbooksonline.com/3-d-printers

*Scanning QR codes requires a web-enabled smart device with a QR code reader app and a camera.

Table of Contents

Chapter 1
3-D Printing 4

Chapter 2
How It Works 8

Chapter 3
Why Print? 12

Chapter 4
The Future of 3-D Printers . 16

Making Connections 22
Glossary 23
Index 24
Online Resources 24

3-D Printing

A 3-D printer can print many different objects. It can print things from glass or metal. It can print things from plastic or chocolate. It can print using many **materials**.

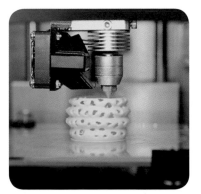

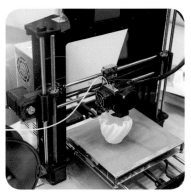

Watch a video here!

You could print toys, bowls, clothes, or airplane parts with a 3-D printer.

3-D printing was invented in the 1980s. The **technology** has gotten better since then. It has become cheaper and more popular.

Some 3-D printers are small enough to fit on tabletops.

Chapter 2

How It Works

All 3-D printers build
objects one layer at a
time. Computer programs
tell them how to make
each layer.

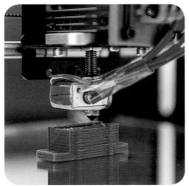

Complete an activity here!

1 A design for a 3-D object is created on a computer program

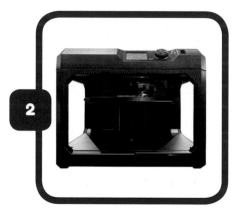

2 The design is sent to a 3-D printer.

3 The 3-D printer heats material and builds the object in thin layers.

The most common 3-D printer has a heater that melts plastic. Then the plastic is squeezed out of a **nozzle** into thin layers. Many layers of plastic form an object.

Chapter 3

Why Print?

Most things are built in **factories**. Parts are cut from material. Leftover material is often wasted.

Learn more here!

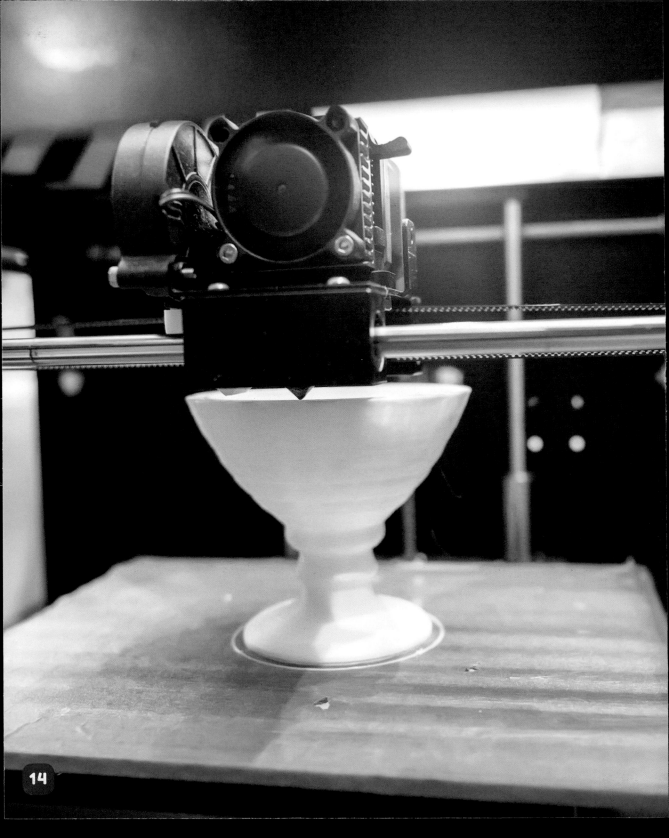

But 3-D printers don't waste material. Their nozzles only squeeze out the amount of material needed to build something.

Chapter 4

The Future of 3-D Printers

People are still learning about what 3-D printers can do. The technology is still changing.

Learn more here!

Today, doctors can 3-D
print simple body parts.

These can replace broken body parts for people who are hurt. Doctors hope this can help more people in the future.

One day, there could be a 3-D printer in every home. You could print your own toys, tools, and clothes. You could choose the color, size, and shape of everything you print.

Some people have used 3-D printers to build whole houses!

Making Connections

Text-to-Self

If you had a 3-D printer in your house, what would you make?

Text-to-Text

Have you read another book about 3-D printing or other modern technology? What did you learn in that book?

Text-to-World

How might 3-D printing change the world?

Glossary

factory – a building where things are made.

material – something that is used to make something else.

nozzle – a short tube that controls the flow of liquid or melted material.

technology – objects created by using science.

Index

chocolate, 4

computers, 8, 10

doctors, 18–19

factories, 12

glass, 4

materials, 4, 12, 15

plastic, 4, 11

technology, 7, 16

Online Resources

popbooksonline.com

Thanks for reading this Cody Koala book!

Scan this code* and others like it in this book, or visit the website below to make this book pop!

popbooksonline.com/3-d-printers

*Scanning QR codes requires a web-enabled smart device with a QR code reader app and a camera.

3931